Cadenza

Copyright © 2000 by Hume Fogg Academic High School.

All rights reserved.

Published by Write Together™ Publishing LLC.
www.writetogether.com

Project Sponsor:
Mr. Bill Brown

Computer Technician:
Chris Michie

Editors:
Melissa Bullock
Sarah Dryden
Abbe Kopra
Sarah Miller

Business Representatives:
Cle'shea Crain
Lina Kharats
D'Andrea Witherspoon
Aliene Howell
Karen Tankersley

Project Design:
Christine Lee
Jennifer Kiilerich
Alisa Loveman

Cover Photograph:
Nathan Foote

Typesetting & Book Design:
Charles King

ISBN 1-930142-50-1 Paperback
ISBN 1-930142-51-X Hardback

Cadenza

The Literary Annual of Hume Fogg

WRITE TOGETHER™ PUBLISHING

Nashville, Tennessee

Cadenza

Cadenza: a
technically
brilliant,
sometimes
improvised solo;
an episodic
departure from
the main theme.

Contents

Introduction . . . *Kirk Alexander* 1

Coming Back . . . *Lina Kharats* 3

My Kindred Soul . . . *Karen Tankersley* 3

Nobody But You . . . *Sarah Dryden* 4

I'm From . . . *Brandy Ratcliff* 6

Headless Horsemen . . . *Gina Vizvary* 8

Shoes . . . *Alisa Loveman* 9

Marathon . . . *Aisha Siebert* 10

1979 . . . *Te'Meka Roberts* 11

Jung-Eun . . . *Christine Lee* 12

Time Falling Fast . . . *Amy Lincoln* 13

Thoughts Before Coffee . . . *Kirk Alexander* 13

The Lipstick Lady and the Iron Man Converse

. . . *Sarah Miller* 14

Rain . . . *John Stringham* 15

Chrysalis Women . . . *Abbe Rose Kopra* 18

This is Fowl . . . *Melissa Bullock* 19

What You Never Told Me . . . *DeAndrea Witherspoon* 20

Backstitch . . . *Sarah Dryden* 21

The Box . . . *Christen Sewell* 22

Fashion Police . . . *Marchello Gray* 24

Tribute to Ella Fitzgerald . . . *Missie Tidwell* 25

Nine Years, Nine Months, and Twenty-three Days
   . . . *Melissa Bullock* 26

Paper Shreds . . . *Aliene Howell* 29

Hailstorm . . . *Abbe Rose Kopra* 36

Too Little, Too Late . . . *Sarah Dryden* 37

Atlanta: My Mother's Black History
   . . . *Che'shea Crain* 38

Jackson . . . *Sarah Miller* 39

At Birth . . . *Andrew Lytle* 40

Shield . . . *Jennifer Kiilerich* 41

Good Googily Moogily Jesus, That's a Nice Hat
   . . . *Melissa Bullock* 42

Innocent Me . . . *Gina Vizvary* 43

Roger . . . *Shaffer Grubb* 44

possum . . . *Ciciley Hoffman* 45

Amanda . . . *Amy Lincoln* 46

Manifesto of What the World Owes Me, Dammit
   . . . *Kirk Alexander* 47

Another Quiet War . . . *Lina Kharats* 48

Sad but True . . . *Missie Tidwell*...................................... *49*

Perchance a Fallacy . . . *Sarah Miller* *50*

The Temptress Smell . . . *Aliene Howell* *56*

Night . . . *Te'Meka Roberts*... *57*

Awakening . . . *Alisa Loveman* *58*

Dreaming in the Hallway . . . *Chris Michie* *59*

Jesica . . . *Brandy Ratcliff*... *60*

For Grandmother . . . *Aisha Siebert* *61*

A Quiet Evening at Home . . . *Shaffer Grubb* *62*

Using Everything . . . *John Stringham*............................ *65*

What Mother Says . . . *Marchello Gray*.......................... *66*

Lauren . . . *Abbe Rose Kopra*.. *67*

Final Concert . . . *Christine Lee* *68*

Fallen Angel . . . *Abbe Rose Kopra*................................... *69*

Temptation . . . *Che'shea Crain*.. *70*

Nightmares . . . *DeAndrea Witherspoon* *71*

"Girl Interrupted" . . . *Jennifer Kiilerich*......................... *72*

Rain vs. Skydivers . . . *Kirk Alexander*............................ *73*

Kids . . . *Andrew Lytle* *74*

Mother and Son in Mali . . . *Karen Tankersley*............... *75*

After Reading the Poem "Concert in the Garden" by Octavio Paz

. . . *Alisa Loveman* *76*

The Willow Tree . . . *Chris Michie* *77*

Grams and St. Jude . . . *Gina Vizvary* *78*

Reflection . . . *Christine Lee* *79*

Room 104 . . . *Marchello Gray* *80*

That Was Then . . . *Cle'shea Crain* *81*

Void of Dreams . . . *Christen Sewell* *82*

Beneath Anger . . . *Karen Tankersley* *83*

Canoe Trip . . . *Chris Michie* *84*

No, I Didn't Go to School Today . . . *Brandy Ratcliff* *85*

Last Days . . . *Te'Meka Roberts* *86*

Courtney . . . *Missie Tidwell* *88*

Janc . . . *Amy Lincoln* *89*

New Light . . . *Andrew Lytle* *90*

My Soul and I . . . *Kirk Alexander* *91*

To My Friend . . . *Jennifer Kiilerich* *92*

Subway . . . *Aisha Siebert* *93*

Lost in St. Petersburg, 1956 . . . *Lina Kharats* *94*

Cheating Time: Sestina for the Eighties

. . . *Sarah Dryden* *96*

Never Go to Florida . . . *Marchello Gray* *98*

Introduction

George Orwell never said, in *1984*, "The theme I'm trying to convey is that losing control of the little things costs." Instead, Orwell wove a narrative and, afterwards, the reader looked beyond the words on the paper and picked up the theme he wanted a reader to understand. Every theme or symbol that is implicitly woven into the text that you find... that is a cadenza. A flourish in the actuality that connects you to life.

The works that follow are rife with cadenzas, and not just with themes. If you look into the work here, you will find not just the images and scenes you could find in any anthology, but also the cadenzas, the flourishes of life at Hume Fogg High School, and the personalities of a very diverse group of people.

This is a collection of pieces from 25 seniors and one junior. I'm not going to tell you about all the things we sacrificed to produce these pieces, all the projects and other homeworks we had to navigate around to find time to make these pieces, because these pieces are not about school, and neither is this book. This book is about a year in the life of 26 people, and it's about life as we see it.

We did not make these words. The words "fish" and "table" and "brown" existed before us, and we learned them, but how we've used them, the ideas they express, are brand new. The finesse, the verve, the flair with which we wove in themes, ideas, and images are the cadenzas in between the words you see and hear.

Kirk Alexander

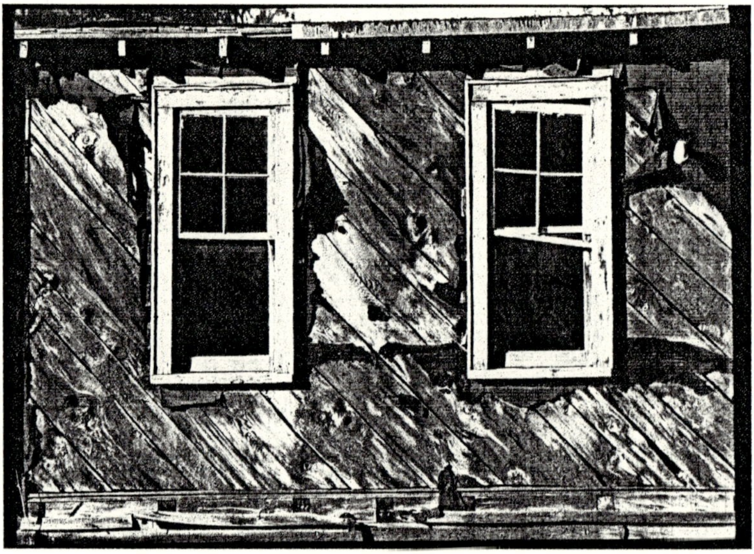

Coming Back

That faint scar on your right temple—
You still reach for it now, twenty years later,
As we sit in an old café in Montmartre
And toast to oblivion.
The dim lamps have not changed,
But we no longer seek to hide white sleepless nights
In their welcoming shadows.
And a broken voice of someone's guitar
Does not linger in this warm summer twilight
With a simple sweet tune
Once in fashion so many twilights ago.
Pretty frivolous dancers
Throw us coy playful glances
From beneath smoky eyelids,
And we watch iridescent beads
Sparkle on their dark bodies,
Coil around girls' necks in voluptuous darkness...
It's silent.
But I know—
You, too, dream of Parisian sunrise.
For cheap wine no longer quenches our thirst
As we sit on colorless chairs in Montmartre
And toast to oblivion.

Lina Kharats

My Kindred Soul

If you let the cool spring water
  glide through your hands
    A thousand miles away
      mine will shiver.

Karen Tankersley

Cadenza

Nobody but You

Five little odes
On Andy Warhol's
Self-Portrait #1

I.
Impersonal.
Silk-screened a thousand times
From a photograph.
Blown up to larger-than-life,
A line separating his face
Into two trapezoids
Of pink and blue.
Super-modern, super-pop,
He made superstars
Of ordinary drag queens
And cokeheads.

II.
Closer, the brushstrokes
Are visible
He quickly,
Almost haphazardly
Slapped the canvas—
Probably distracted
By someone trying
To leech more out of him—
His boundless generosity
Never enough for them.

III.
His mouth points down
At the corners,
Dejected by the trust
That Valerie Solanas shot out of him.
Lips still upturned

Still dewy and innocent,
But they're all sucking him dry.
Eyes squint a little,
Black-circled,
Pained by the tight corset
That keeps his insides in.

IV.
Half pink, half blue
Androgynous.
Platinum blond
Beautiful, delicate
Like a teenage virgin.
Porcelain-pale like the eggshells
His mother painted for him.
The artist everyone loved to hate
"His 15 minutes are up,"
Admonished the gods of the art world,
"Anyone who can work a silkscreen
Can do what he does."

V.
But no one can do what he did.
Anyone can wallpaper a room
In Reynolds Wrap,
But no one can love and trust and give
So unflinchingly.
Anyone can cut-and-paste
Polaroids of Mick Jagger and Jackie O.,
But nobody else's camera
Could capture raw, naked soul.
Anybody can smear acrylics
On giant canvases screened
With pictures of Chanel bottles,
But who else would have thought of it?

Sarah Dryden

Cadenza

I'm From

Colorado possessed majestic mountains,
rock formations that broke the sky,
shattering the clouds into a million pieces.
Horrible dry air, barely breathable,
wet fields of blue-violet wildflowers.
A bustling city,
rude traffic,
poorly constructed apartment buildings
rundown K-marts and King Soopers.
Just across the line of suburbia,
everything is French,
chalets and chateaux.
Cool aqua waterslides and hell-fire heat.
Stinking lakeside,
sticky sand in my sandals.
"Dig in your heels."
I only sat under a tree, staring at the sky.
Grandma and Grandpa gutted the fish
while I sat with a blank mind.
I just want to go home.

In Missouri the grass was puke brown,
never a lovely shade, not even in the springtime.
Litter packs into colonies along the sidewalk and in the street,
running alongside tattered, paint-chipped mailboxes,
houses covered with tarps to keep the rain out.
Once-white sidewalks are yellowed with the vagabond footprint.
There's only one tiny window in the apartment.
He peers down at the populace;
they move with a synchronized footfall,
blank gazes, black eyes,
no reactions, hopeless.

Cadenza

They're cold like the basement floor,
the icy ceiling,
chains dangling from the pipes.
He steps off a chair and ends the footfall of slavery.

Tennessee is hot summers, frozen winters,
foggy windshields in the dawn,
shooing wild hares from my rear tires.
The city of my mourning childhood.
My doors are locked forever.
I hate you,
I hate mom,
I hate my teachers,
I hate my beautiful classmates,
my fat face,
my cold sores,
my childish impurity.
Watching the wallpaper ripple and morph,
breathing like pools of water.
My Barbie Dreamhouse torn down,
she's lying stripped down with her head shaven,
staring at the walls of her bedroom.
Time heals,
summers in the park,
daisies smiling up at my matured face,
nights at the café with a cool breeze and a mocha latte,
but I still hate everyone.

Brandy Ratcliff

Cadenza

Headless Horsemen
—Sleepy Hollow Cemetery, New York

Mary comes to the cemetery to
listen to the stories woven in
the green leaves.

Asphalt roads stretch out like veins, but
she walks on the grass.
The crunching reminds her that she's alive.

The legend of Sleepy Hollow reflects in the
brook that flows under the forbidden bridge.
Unlike Ichabod, she will cross unharmed.

Mary comes to the cemetery so her
headless horsemen can't follow.
Instead, they fade into the stones and the
little signs that tell her she can't fish here.

She lingers amongst the deer
and the familiar slate names.
She waves to the gatekeeper,
whose real purpose is unknown.

Dusk falls and she retraces her path.
Her last foot steps off the bridge.
The horsemen slink out of the stones.

Hollow cries of horses

The chase is on

Gina Vizvary

Shoes

Cloudy eyes peer from a broken shoebox.
They've walked so long
they don't even remember how to blink.
Don't believe I'll ever see like I used to.
People say it's no problem, I can get a new pair.
But I don't want a new pair.
I like the holes where the heels should have been—
puts me on some kind of a tilt,
always have to look up,
never have to see the craziness around me.
Maybe the heel wore out first because
I put too much weight on the past.
The past stays with me like a pair of dirty socks.
At least they match.
I miss my old sandals,
shoes like a second skin,
weren't even shoes anymore.
New sandals look too sterile and have a shiny glare.
The ground is too flat,
and the straps fit tightly around my toes,
telling me they are here for good—
but nothing's permanent.
I'll walk all over them and show them the streets
until they, too, will wear in the heel
and start to tilt upward,
only wanting to see the sky.

Alisa Loveman

Cadenza

Marathon

    The sound of feet hitting pavement echoes in his ears. A thin tank top flaps against his frail ribcage, a steady heartbeat pumping out the pace. In the distance he can see a bend in the course.... If I can make it around this corner, I'll be all right. Thoughts of Friday night slip into his head, sitting around a bar as friends drown their problems in bottomless glasses, and you try to give that fine girl in the corner a sly smile when you can barely hold yourself up. What did she say her name was? Shane, Shanna...it really doesn't matter. Tomorrow, there'll be another one sitting there, waiting for a guy to pick her up. There always is. The bartender watches the clock. He looks pissed as hell; I'm sure he has somewhere better to be than here, refilling glasses for a bunch of drunk college students. Five years from now, they'll come in with suits and briefcases, maybe leave a little extra in the tip because they vaguely remember the guy behind the counter. But tonight, they lie passed out on the floor while he calls a cab to take them home.... Isn't life great? The next part is a blur. I only remember being bent over a toilet, watching the water swirl round and round, making me dizzy. On my knees in a dirty bathroom stall, trying to remember how many times I've done this. I want to tell it over again. I want to wake up that morning and decide to do something with my life.... Maybe I will. A voice comes over the loudspeaker as runner number 137 rounds the corner: "Mile marker fifteen." Only a few more to go....

Aisha Siebert

Cadenza

1979

As the days turn into nights,
I will be here waiting.
1979.
I cried, but you said that you had to go.
Called to serve the beautiful.
It was the coldest day in June.
My tears froze the sky,
and hardened my cheek,
as they ran.
Your hand was
the only object of warmth.
But its fiery feel
could not warm my chilled body.
I shiver,
When I think of the stalactites
that hang from my heart.
I feel a pain
so cold
that it can only be warmed
by the hands of Hell.

Te'Meka Roberts

Cadenza

Jung-Eun

You are adorable when you get mad at me.
You aggravate me so much
My thoughts become incomprehensible.
I love it when you come into my room every day
To bother me,
To tell me about people you know,
What you think of school and the weather
And the cartoon Sailor Moon
That we love more than anyone else.
We revel in memories, old times
When our dolls really were our children,
How we possessed incredible magical powers
And could manipulate the flow of time
By pressing the rewind button in the air.
Our utopia was called Vanilla World
Where animals were happy citizens
Where the states were all made of chocolate
And strawberry ice cream.
We dance frantically to Korean rap music
That is slightly too sugary
And lip sync with passion
Because our voices are like our parents'.
We watch stupid Disney movies
That never made it to the big screen.
You're the only one that will play
Trivial Pursuit with me.
You cause me more guilt than anyone else
When I hurt you.
And this is only the beginning of reasons
That show why I love you.

Christine Lee

Time Falling Fast

I come from strawberry frosted donuts on Sunday mornings,
A mid-afternoon swim at Horse's Heaven or Deep Rocks,
A night spent with a sleeping bag and a tent in the backyard,
Sitting on the dock, feet in the cool water of Lake St. Catherine.

I come from midnight mass in Marblehead on Christmas Eve,
A boat ride out to a sandbar near Plum Island or Crane's Beach,
Pizza and a visit to Little Nana's brown house in Gloucester,
An evening walk to the post office on Main Street in Rowley.

I come from a stone-wall shortcut to school with my best
    friend Elizabeth,
Singing loudly and swimming around the living room like a
    mermaid,
Throwing Rosy in the air and catching her before she hits
    the ground,
Shuffling around a century-old school building, letting my
    time run out.

Amy Lincoln

Thoughts Before Coffee

Whoever is knocking on my door
you'd best be here with a note
telling me that I'm now a Saint,
or legally dead,
because those seem the only
two things that could possibly
motivate me to throw back these
covers after the crap I called
yesterday.
I would also accept a million dollars.

Kirk Alexander

Cadenza

The Lipstick Lady and the Iron Man Converse

Stuffy statue of a man who saved men by killing others,
all-purpose iron form symbolizes the nondescript
termination machine.
Were he alive, he would have snubbed
the advances of the Lipstick Lady,
lifted his rusty lip in a well-practiced sneer
at the first sight of her tattered apparel.
Grimaced, inwardly, at the odor of her mold-covered shopping bag.
He would have gawked outright, though, when he saw the bright
Passion Pink lipstick that encircled her mouth in a wide ellipse,
traversing the wrinkles of her worn face to its far reaches.
The sole reminder of her high-school regality
(prom queen of '66).
"How you?" she drawls.
He stares.
"Is that so?" she inquires, kindly.
He ignores her.
"Don't have to be so huffy," she snaps, and then,
by way of retribution, she places her half-smoked cigarette
in his unflinching hand.
"They always do," she replies, understandingly.
He doesn't deserve her.

Sarah Miller

Rain

Rain slowly ran down the windowpane, tiny drops that joined together, traveled down for a while, then separated, two once again. The street, down the hill from the gray stone house, shimmered with the passing of every vehicle, changing from dark, tarnished silver to a brilliant gold, then back to dull sterling. Adam stood at the window, staring out into the dreary landscape of his front yard, of his street. He stood, staring straight ahead, looking at everything, yet seeing nothing. Change was so difficult, yet it was for the best. Adam ran his fingers through his hair, silver at the temples, distinguished-looking. He sighed as his eyes followed a blue sedan slithering across the wet asphalt in front of him.

"Adam, could you come help me? I can't move this desk by myself." Adam set his glass down on a pile of boxes and followed that voice out the study door. That voice, gentle and musical, could always lift his spirits whenever he heard it. Adam walked down the hall and up the stairs, finding his wife in the second floor hall struggling with a large secretary in vain.

"It took you long enough. Grab an end and help me get it downstairs." Jenny gestured to an end, then gripped the desk. Slowly the two waddled down the hall. By the time they reached the stairs, both needed a short break.

Jenny furrowed her brow, "You holding up okay?"

"Yeah, just fine." Adam's voice was indifferent, "Ready to give it another try?" The two labored to find a grip and wrestle the piece of furniture down the stairs. They worked wordlessly, anticipating each other's needs and responding before the other could ask for assistance. Finally the two got the monstrosity down the stairs and to the front door. Through the door a U-Haul truck stood, the back open and already filled with numerous boxes, chairs, the odds and ends of daily life. The two dragged the desk inside the truck, struggling to make it fit into that spatial jigsaw puzzle. Once it was wedged in place, Adam used his sleeve to wipe the rain from the antique walnut.

"I always liked this piece,"

Cadenza

"Yes, it is nice. Well, shall we continue?" Jenny walked inside, small black spots appearing on her navy T-shirt where raindrops had hit. She grabbed an empty box from the hall, walked upstairs. Adam stared after her. Slowly he realized he was still outside, getting soaked, and, with a grunt, he walked inside and back to the study.

He returned to work, placing books and pictures into cardboard boxes. A lifetime of memories housed by corrugated cardboard. The wedding picture. Jenny in her white dress, a radiant smile graced her lips. Her hair cascaded down her neck and shoulders, one strand out of place, over her left eye. Adam stood behind her, his hand on her waist, stealing a sideways glance at her. Adam remembered the day he had brought her to this house. Jenny had stepped out of the car, mouth agape. It was a beautiful house. She looked at Adam lovingly, tears in her eyes, whispered, "It's wonderful." He scooped her up and carried her through the door. The happiest moment of his life. He was near her.

Adam stopped work, turned back to the window. The sky was still dark, the trees still swaying in the wind. Rain continued to fall on the roof; rain continued to run down the pane of glass. Tires on the road made a gentle rushing sound as they passed the house. After today, nothing would ever be the same.

Jenny walked into the room. "These the last of the boxes?"

"Yeah." Adam was suddenly tired. This had been a taxing experience, packing up life, getting ready to start over. The fatigue had finally caught up with him. He hadn't been sleeping at night.

"All right. I'll get them." Jenny bent down to pick up the two boxes. As she straightened up, the top box, the one Adam had just packed, fell to the floor. Books flopped out. The glass in picture frames tinkled on the hardwood. The wedding picture fell at Adam's feet, cracked glass spiderwebbing across that moment. He knelt down, started to pick it up, maybe it could be fixed. Jenny reached in, grabbed it, picked up the shards of glass, the broken ceramic figurines, and threw them all into the wastebasket. Adam slowly picked up books; Jenny returned from the other side of the room to help. They worked in silence, repacking the box, until they both reached for the same book. Their hands touched. Adam looked into Jenny's eyes. She looked away and withdrew her hand.

The spilled box was repackaged. Adam carried it to the rental truck, placed it beside the huge desk, and returned to the porch. Jenny stood there, putting on her forest green rain jacket, hiding her brown curls with the hood. As he climbed the steps, Adam said, "Is that everything?"

"Yes, I think so." Jenny's eyes stared past Adam, to the wet road beyond the front yard. Those eyes had always haunted Adam. Blue and deep, he used to get lost staring into them as they talked. He was hypnotized. Those blue eyes shifted from the road to Adam. "Well, I ... I guess I'm off."

Adam was silent for about thirty seconds. Lately silence had become a blanket to him. He would often sit alone in the house, no noise besides the gentle ticking of the grandfather clock in the hall, slow and rhythmic.

Adam cleared his throat. Forced words escaped his lips, barely audible over the slow hiss of rain. "I suppose you'll be back next week with the papers for me to sign?"

"No, I'll just drop them in the mail." Jenny passed by him, leaving the dry porch, stepping onto the rain-soaked driveway. Adam's hand reached out and touched her shoulder. Jenny stopped, her back toward him.

Adam coughed. "It's slick out there. Be careful." He dropped his hand.

Jenny continued walking to the cab of the truck. She opened the door and stepped inside. A short minute passed before the engine rumbled to life and the U-Haul slowly crept down the driveway. It entered the street, its headlights reflecting gold onto the dull sterling of the asphalt. The truck lumbered down the road, around the bend, and out of sight.

Adam entered the house. The hall echoed with his footsteps. He walked to the study, turned to the window. Adam could see his reflection in the glass. Raindrops crawled down the mirrored cheeks. In the hall, the grandfather clock struck one.

John Stringham

Cadenza

Chrysalis Women

She has a dark ponytail and a shiny forehead.
Bending among the carefully stacked piles of laundry,
She watches her rough hands move quickly,
automatically.

    The pulsating beat resonates in her hips.
    Swinging around the cheap brass pole
    She skims her hands down her body,
    Eyes flashing with mock hunger
    at the man at her ankles,
    bald and grinning.

The show is a rerun,
blaring in a corner.
Canned laughter swells around her.
The slender young actress has thighs of perfection.
"A TV housewife," the woman thinks.
She sets another folded handkerchief in its proper place
and smoothes her hands over her bulging hips.

    A bony foot in a stiletto shoe
    Rises from the garden of beer bottles.
    Budweiser, Michelob, long pale leg.
    Whistles and cheering erupt as she bends low,
    shimmies back up,
    a wave of nubile young flesh
    and tousled blond hair.

The kitchen timer is shrieking.
She pulls the tray of chicken nuggets from the oven,
puts one between her lips,
chews slowly.

Her knees ache as she climbs down from the table.
The bar is deserted and twice as ugly
at four in the morning.
Limp ones and fives feel sweaty in her hands.
Looking into the cracked bathroom mirror,
she makes a promise to her tired blue eyes.
Tomorrow it ends.

Lying awake she hears his thick snoring.
She is careful to observe the quarantine effected
since she gained the weight.
He could have left, she reminds herself.
She'd burnt the pie
and broken a plate.
White knuckles clutch the edge of the sheet.
Tomorrow.
Tomorrow she'll do better.

Abbe Rose Kopra

This is Fowl

Chickens and I,
we have a lot in common.
Try as we might
we just can't seem
to get off the ground.
I flap my stubby little arms.
They flap their stubby little wings.
And we jump.
And we come crashing down
onto the ground.
Then a farmer comes and tries to cut off our heads.

Melissa Bullock

Cadenza

What You Never Told Me

I remember that night.
It was a cold November;
the air seemed to
break through my skin.
You convinced me
to run away with you.
As I jumped inside
the '67 Chevy,
throwing my bag
in the back seat,
I didn't have
a care in the world.
We drove without a map,
it was crazy.
We stopped in an old cafe
off Highway 70
and shared old stories
over hazelnut coffee—
your favorite.
We watched cars drive by
and laughed at people.
Then, there was silence.
I asked why you were so quiet.
You leaned over
to kiss my forehead
and told me you
were dying.
I cracked a smile
and didn't believe you.
You're too young I said.
You told me to forget about it
and I did, for you.

I never went home
that night
because I never left.
We never went to the
old cafe, and
you never told me
you were dying
I had to hear it
from someone else.

DeAndrea Witherspoon

Backstitch
For Jason

Your needle-eye psyche
Never failed to frustrate me.
Talking to you was like trying
To put double-thick hemp rope
Through that one tiny
Gold-plated opening:
An eye that squeezed shut
On everything I had to say.
I hit you in the face with my words,
Tried to force them through—
But there was no way
I could ever pierce your skull.
The threads split and unraveled
Upon meeting the end of your nose
So that I had to cut them short
And try again
Until my statements became fragmented,
Clipped little bits of thread
That couldn't sew you back together.

Sarah Dryden

Cadenza

The Box

I invited you over to play.
I showed you to my secret chest,
Full of treasures:
My favorite baby doll, Abby Elizabeth,
The things I swore to love forever,
A book, whose cover is now removable—
It's been read so many times.
I was sure you felt honored,
For I hadn't shared the contents with anyone.

Soon, you weren't sharing.
You were taking, taking,
Until my box was empty.

Then you returned to my box
And reacted with surprise
When you saw the wasteland.
My cherished secrets, gone.
All that's left is a limb from a Barbie doll,
The lock to my diary,
A dried-out marker.

Oh, but you could fix it.
You filled my box with substitutes:
A button from a jacket you gave me.
The thin wire from the necklace
I once wore in your honor.
A pair of glasses you don't need
Because you don't look at me anymore.
A candy wrapper.
A banana peel.
A slap in the face.

Cadenza

You thought I'd be like new.
You thought you'd made amends—
Filled my treasured chest with
Ugly reminders of what you stole.

And now when others come along
And see the cheap contents,
They pity my poor state.
Never taking a second glance
To see if perhaps the contents of my box
Could be made good again.

At the doctor's office they always say
This will never hurt.
Your trust in them is soon lost
When you're left with the sting of a needle.
You, too, have left me with a wound
No band-aid can heal.
You walked away with my heart
And gave me a lollipop.

Christen Sewell

Cadenza

Fashion Police

Wouldn't it be great if a huge alarm went off
when somebody walked in the room wearing plaid stretch
   pants and a striped sweater
or if people could get citations for wearing high waters or
   having bad crotch tucks
or wedgies or zippers held together with a clothespin.
It would be great if there were policemen on duty giving tickets
to people in bright green FUBU jackets
or basketball shoes with tapered leg jeans.
The country would be safer if the major police code was not 187,
but 817...a D.W.I....dressing without instruction.
Everyday cops could chase down people wearing those baggy
   MC Hammer suits
or jeans with blazers and especially cardigan sweaters.
Things like turtlenecks and flannel shirts would be basic misdemeanors;
offenders would simply have to watch a short film or pay a fee.
Social Security would go toward educating older people on
   new fashions,
like wearing cotton instead of polyester and giving anatomical
   lessons
reminding them where their waists are in relation to their chests.
The SWAT team would only be necessary in extreme cases
where fat, fat women find their way into Victoria's Secret
or start believing that bigger is really better and begin
   revealing themselves.
Repeat offenders would be sent to some type of rehabilitation
where they are brainwashed with J. Crew catalogs
or that GAP commercial where they "call him Mello Yello."
Special hygiene units could be called in
to deal with people with those permanent yellow pit stains
or skid marks, and to put an end to dandruff once and for all.
The possibilities of this idea are endless,
and it would put an end to the madness plaguing our streets
   each day.

Marchello Gray

Cadenza

Tribute to Ella Fitzgerald

She belts out tunes to hundreds
at the Cotton Club,
while I croak to my mirror
into a cotton swab.

In my lungs, her
"Fascinating Rhythm,"
isn't quite so interesting and her
"Lover, come back to me,"
never grants me success.

She caramel-coated
any song by the Duke
and could hit that
with her skit skat.

She poured over the stage,
exuding radiance from
shiny black folds of skin.
All the while,
sounding like honey
dripping through the fingers
she had everyone wrapped around.

She was certainly
"Marvelous,
too Marvelous for Words."

Missie Tidwell

Cadenza

Nine years, Nine months, and Twenty-three days

    Lining out the years
on paper—
one year for one line—
your life
takes up not even ten.
    My sister,
        a year, a month, a day
        younger than me,
        has been dead six years now.
    I remember that day;
as sole family witness, I was
reciting again and again
how you ran across
and the car came
from nowhere.
Leaving out my screams for the
neighbor who was a nurse.
Leaving out my commands of Tess—
only eight then—to get mom, to get dad.
Leaving out me kneeling next to you,
looking down at you.
I remember thinking I could—
I should do something more.
    Mom returned that night
to tell Tess and me
you were in a coma,
your right leg was broken.
    The next day at school
I left class,
called four different
numbers to reach three
different sections of Vanderbilt Hospital.
The fourth got me mom—

Cadenza

surprised a ten-year-old could
navigate convoluted phone lines.
The next three days I repeated
the process—leaving class and
calling the waiting room
to see if you had awoken.
I never believed you wouldn't.
    Friday, I remember,
getting off the bus, I saw Grandma—
there to pick me up
and take me to the hospital.
I knew on the way there
you were gone.
I was quiet.
I asked about Tess.
    We pulled up and got out.
Took the elevator.
There were Mr. Kerry and Tess.
Grandmothers and Grandfathers.
I joined Tess
And mom appeared.
    "Kate's dead."
        "She's dead?"
    "She just died."
I remember Mr. Kerry
hugging Dad.
I remember Grandma
taking me to the bathroom and leaving me.
I looked into the mirror,
washed my face, returned.
Took Tess to the bathroom.
Mom asked if we wanted
to see you—but we
had to be quiet.

Cadenza

Walking into the Children's ICU
I glanced around,
then saw you.
Tubes disconnected.
Eyes closed.
I touched your face.
I watched others touch you.
We were ushered out
and sent home.
    Tess and I, we
went to your room—
held your things.
Tess took your lion.
We went to the playhouse—
to be alone,
to be together.
I told Tess
the next bunny she saw—
that would be you watching over her.
She did always look up to you.
    I remember the funeral.
I remember thinking I saw your chest moving.
I remember knowing I saw your chest moving.
I remember the tears.
    Six years later
I space your life
on paper—not
even ten lines.
I remember.

Melissa Bullock

Paper Shreds

The sun striped the room through Venetian blinds, waking Virginia from her dreams. She blinked her eyes at the sun's glare from between Barbie sheets. She realized her mom had forgotten to wake her for the school bus, so Virginia changed out of flannel pajamas and into a soft, blue shirt and faded jeans. She washed her face in the bathroom to wake up, and then rushed to the kitchen for a bowl of Cheerios. She put homework and a peanut butter and jelly sandwich in her pink backpack before she hurried out the door.

On the two-mile walk to school she contemplated another excuse for tardiness. She hated it when her mother did this. Her face grimaced as she remembered the disheveled image lying on the couch. The faded lipstick and drippy mascara were almost covered by the hair that had come uncurled. Mom used to take her to the parties, but mostly Virginia remembered the flat beer and conversations. She shuddered at the thought of all the women in dresses and the men with wandering eyes as she pulled her cap down lower to hide from the memory.

She knew her mom would pick her up after school with some kind of special candy, or if she felt really guilty, it'd be a snow globe. Virginia loved the snow globes and had built up a small collection, but she really just wanted someone to make eggs and toast for her. She enviously imagined what her friends had eaten for breakfast or what types of special treats were in their neatly packed lunches. She got her shield ready, prepared to fight the questions; today it would be the car that broke down, she hadn't used that one in a while. Her unbrushed hair blew across her face in the wind and she wiped it from her mouth with a small hand. Virginia pulled her jacket tighter and convinced herself that Mom loved her, even though she forgot sometimes.

The looming metal doors to the elementary school spoke of the oncoming embarrassment. She opened the large door and stepped inside with tired legs. The heat felt good but did nothing to relax her body as she stepped into the office to sign in late.

Cadenza

One of the nice ladies in the office gave her a strange look, and Virginia mumbled the excuse she had practiced to precision. The woman stood up, hulking over her with short graying hair. She walked Virginia to Mrs. Allen's second grade class and Virginia noticed the hole that was starting to emerge on the lady's shoe. The floor had many scuffs and abrasions, like the ones Mom had always gotten mad at her for putting on the kitchen tiles. She kept looking at them until finally she reached the doorway to the classroom. It opened with a gentle push from the strange haired lady. In they walked, but Virginia watched the floor although she could feel the twenty-two pairs of eyes piercing her.

She did not look up until she realized she was being tugged by Mrs. Allen towards the corner. "I'm sorry I'm late again, Mrs. Allen. My mom's car broke down," she mumbled quietly, sure that was to be the topic of conversation. She dared to steal a glance into the teacher's deep-set eyes, but timidly returned her face downward.

"Are you sure that's what happened? Because you can tell me if it was anything else. I won't be mad."

Virginia continued to stare at the floor, not wanting to reveal the lifestyle of her mother, but knowing she should tell the truth. The more the battle raged inside her, the more interesting the scuffmarks on the floor became.

"You can tell me, it's okay. I won't tell your mom what you say." Mrs. Allen noticed how the last part of her speech had caught the child's attention. She looked up in a frightened trance but her body began to relax a little. Virginia just stared for a moment and finally began to stutter something scarcely audible.

The teacher couldn't understand, and so she leaned down next to the young girl's body. Virginia couldn't say it a second time, loyalty and fear of her mother kept the secret hidden. She just told Mrs. Allen that she had to walk to school today since the car was broken down and she didn't feel well. Understanding the child's need for peace, the teacher yielded from the subject and told Virginia to lie down on the beanbags in the corner of the room.

Freed from the pressure of lies, she relaxed and let the blue nylon stick to her skin as her eyes closed in relaxation. Now, everything would be okay for a while. After ten minutes of reassurance, she meandered back to the green rug where all the students were sitting. Her friend Kara whispered to Virginia the assignment. They had to make Mother's Day cards. As Virginia cut the heart out of the pink construction paper she thought about why she loved her mother. The biggest reason she could think of was that Mom hadn't left her like her father. She could barely remember him. Just the way his big hands felt, and how his brown hair fell across his eyes. She tried not to think about him, but whenever she went into Mom's room there was a cracked picture frame on the nightstand of the three of them. Sometimes she still saw her mother clutching the picture.

A tap on the shoulder released Virginia from the memories as Mrs. Allen asked about her mother again. She wanted to know what she loved about her mother.

"I love the way she holds me when I have nightmares... and... when she makes pancakes for me on Sundays."

Mrs. Allen was reassured by this answer, since she had noticed the girl's card was still blank inside. The teacher quieted her suspicion and figured Virginia had just been distracted somehow.

Virginia's card was almost done when it was time to go home, so she stuffed it in her backpack, determined to finish later. She anxiously ran outside, eager to see her mother. She couldn't spot the red Honda but she kept looking, refusing to be disappointed again. A couple of minutes later she found it and sprinted to her mother's car. The door opened and there was a man inside wearing a pinstriped business suit.

"Mona, I mean, your mom, is still at work. She came in late and hasn't finished yet. She said to ask you if you'd rather go home or come back to work with her. She told me to pick you up in her car so that you wouldn't get confused."

She wanted to see her mother despite the humming lights and sterile smell of her workplace. She climbed into the car and beyond "take me to work" she rode the rest of the way in silence. Virginia remembered how much she detested the ugly framed posters that adorned her mother's office building. By the time

Cadenza

they parked and made it to the front door of Johnson, Yates, & Harrison, Inc. she was regretting her decision to come.

The elevator attendant smiled at her and handed her a lollipop as they rose through the building. He had seen the child before and remembered what a beautiful smile she had given him the last time he handed her a sucker. Virginia thanked the man, and being quite delighted with the watermelon blow-pop in her mouth, she forgot about her mom until the elevator doors opened.

"Hey baby!" her mom squealed as she caught sight of Virginia. Virginia ran to her and climbed into her mother's lap, yet not forgetting her anger, pouted and crossed her arms.

"I know. I'm so sorry about this morning and not picking you up after school. It was Erin's birthday last night, you remember Erin don't you? Well, all the girls went out for drinks to celebrate, and I meant to come home early, but…um…I got you a snow globe on my lunch break. And how bout if we get ice cream after dinner tonight."

Virginia eagerly grasped the new toy and slowly turned it upside down and back upright, watching each flake drop to the bottom. She couldn't help but be pleased with the promise for ice cream, though it would not appease her anger. She began to wiggle and squirm, becoming more anxious to go home.

"How much longer?" Virginia whined. Her mother just smiled and told her a minute more.

The man who had picked Virginia up spoke out in a slightly condescending voice that made it obvious he wasn't used to children. "Your mommy works hard to be a good paralegal. Do you know what par-ah-lee-gul means?"

Virginia just rolled her eyes and retreated to a chair in the back of the office. She played with her snow globe until it was time for them to leave. She raced her mom to the car with her backpack banging against her back. When they made it home, Virginia thought their couch had never looked so welcoming. She turned on the television while her mom put dinner in the microwave. Just as the last beep signaled a hot dinner, the phone rang and Virginia leapt from the couch to answer it. It was for her mother, but Virginia thought the voice sounded a lot like

Mrs. Allen's. She went back to watching the television show, but she could still hear her mother's side of the conversation from her spot on the couch.

"Yes, I know Virginia was tardy again today."

"Why? Oh…. um…She had a check up at the dentist today."

"Car…huh? No, my car's not in the shop, it's fine. No problems at all."

"Virginia said that? Oh…well…we got a flat tire on the way to school from the appointment, but I fixed it and it's fine now. That's probably what she was thinking of." Virginia winced at this and ran upstairs into her room before she heard anymore. She lay down on her bed and played with her favorite snow globe of the ones her mother had gotten her. The snow falling soothed her somehow. Her mother had told her the snow was just little pieces of shredded paper, but Virginia still liked to imagine herself inside it. It always fascinated her how when she shook it the snow would fall, but then when it settled, the globe looked just as it did before, although each of the particles settled in different places.

She heard the padding of her mother's feet come up the stairs and Virginia felt her stomach sink, wondering what the conversation ahead of her would hold. Her mother knocked on the door as she walked in.

"Virginia, that was your teacher. She's worried about you and she thinks I'm not taking good enough care of you. I told her we were fine and how much I love you. I'm really sorry about what happened this morning. If it happens again, I want you to tell Mrs. Allen that you had a doctor's appointment, all right. Don't worry about a thing, okay. Now how about we go eat that dinner before it gets cold."

"Mom, I don't like being late to school. Stay here at night, okay?"

"I promise, Virginia. You were such a good girl this morning. If we're going to Baskin Robbins after dinner, we better go eat…"

With every bite Virginia thought more of ice cream. She ate quickly while trying to decide which flavor she was going to get. She looked over at her mom after she finished her meal, but her mother was still slowly forking food into her mouth. While Virginia was deciding whether a waffle cone or a sugar cone would go better with her mint chocolate chip ice cream, the doorbell rang. She looked at her mother, who urged her to go answer it.

"It's probably just one of my friends, go ahead and get it, Virginia."

She looked through the peephole and saw that it was that annoying guy from her mom's job that had picked her up.

"Come in. She's over there." He stepped around Virginia, leaving her in a trail of cologne. She wondered if he had more gel in his hair or starch in his shirt. She did not want to share her mother with him.

"Ohhh, Bradley, why are you here tonight?" Virginia hated the voice her mother used when she talked to him.

"Remember that case you were working on today? Well, the client called in and there's been some huge changes made to it. We really need you to type the changes now so that it'll be ready for tomorrow's meeting.'

"Oh my goodness, I hadn't even realized what day it was. Just wait a couple minutes and let me go get ready." Her mother soon re-emerged with make up on and a necklace she put on that Virginia's dad had given to her.

"Oh, Virginia, I'm sorry about ice cream. It looks like I have to go in right away. As soon as I come back we'll go. I don't think it'll be too long." With that she kissed Virginia on the forehead and closed the door behind her before Virginia could protest.

Virginia couldn't handle this one. Her mother didn't usually mess up twice in one day. This could not happen ever again. She stomped around the house screaming louder in each room than the last. She found the card she had worked so hard on for her mother and crumpled it, shoving the card deep into her pocket. Virginia resolved to yell at her as soon as she came home. She was going to wait up, no matter how late, so she could tell her mother right away how furious she was. Virginia was finally going to let out all the emotions that had been festering inside her. She punched her pillow a few times, still in a fit of rage and stormed around the house before silently collapsing into a chair.

After wiping her wet cheeks, Virginia decided the easiest way to stay up was to watch television. She checked the clock on the VCR every fifteen minutes. Despite Virginia's fury, time overcame her and she drifted into sleep. Virginia's mother came home soon after and seeing her daughter soundly asleep she tiptoed into the kitchen and delicately laid the ice cream cones in the freezer.

Virginia didn't wake up until late the next morning, but as soon as she did she marched to her mother's room and saw her curled up in the covers in a deep sleep. She did not falter in her resolution, and sat by her mother's bed until she awoke. An hour and a half later, Mona stirred and somehow Virginia couldn't bear to unload her emotions on her tired mother

Despite her softened outlook on her mother, she still felt the turbulent emotions as vigorously as the night before. Virginia remembered the card in her pocket and took it out. She looked it over slowly and quietly ripped it, letting the pieces fall down on her mother. She went back to her room and started playing with her favorite snow globe and started crying again. She threw the globe across the room and let it shatter on the wall and the little pieces of paper slinked into the carpet.

Mona awoke to the thud, and discovered the card. She tried to piece it together, like the cracked picture on her nightstand. When she realized what it was, she felt just as empty as the card. Virginia and her mother, settled in different places, picked up their shredded paper and cried.

Aliene Howell

Cadenza

Hailstorm

Pungent scent of Lemon Pledge
Allegiance to the crown
Of daffodils that rest upon her head
Lights flash the sirens wail
And die upon the sand
That sifts between my toes
And falls to worlds that no one knows.
A spinning fuchsia whirlpool
Of sequined belly dancers
Where peaceful blue-green dolphins thrive
And leapfrog ever after.
The sweetness of the candy corn
Can only be surpassed
By the wonder-smile on his face
But even love can't last.
The pitter-patter of the drops
Of charm fall at your feet.
Alas! The savory turns to dust
Like burned Rice Krispy Treat.
Long and curling locks of gold
To cover aching mind
And shield the precious innocent
From thought so unrefined.
For love of God! Ye baby-men!
Detested progeny
Of the vile predatory beast
Christened thus: HOMOGENY.
Spurn the stars, they twinkle so...
Why, near unevenly!
For shame, they cry, please cover such
Grotesque obscenity.

Cadenza

The flames lick high, grow restless
Sparking bloody mutiny
Among the mass of wretched coals
So quick to make believe.
And the shining of our godlike sun
Sends soothing warmth, and light,
To save us from the mysteries
Of unfamiliar night.

Abbe Rose Kopra

Too Little, Too Late

All I have left is that one awful picture
Taken on St. Patrick's Day.
Your eyes are half-closed,
Your lips strangely contorted, caught mid-syllable
By the camera.
You're wearing a purple shirt
With an index card taped to it
That says "green."
And one little piece of your hair
Hangs in your eyes.
That's the way I remember you
If I don't think about it very hard.
If I do think,
I know that my knife still stings
Between your shoulder blades,
The wound as raw
As if it were new.
I was stupid, and I'm sorry.
If I could find you now I'd dress your wounds.
You'd take the guilt from my chest like a shirt.
If I knew where you were.

Sarah Dryden

Cadenza

Atlanta
My Mother's Black History

Here stands Georgia—
my Atlanta,
where in the 1940s,
my father couldn't
get a job
because he was
colored.

"Colored" is a funny name
for black people.
It sounds like God
took a brown crayon
and shaded us in.

I remember when
the white man
at the corner store
wouldn't let my mother
buy sugar.
I wondered why,
but somehow already knew.

I knew because it
was the reason
I couldn't drink
from the water fountain
that read, "WHITE"
in block letters above it.

Cadenza

It was the reason
my father spent most nights
on our front step smoking,
cursing the white men
who had turned him away,
not because he wasn't qualified,
but because he was dark,
colored in by God's hands.

Cle'shea Crain

Jackson

My brother left last night, finally on his own at twenty-two.
He packed his little car to its bursting point,
pecked me on the cheek, and drove towards Manchester.
I cried as I watched him go, not because he can't
make it in the world,
but because this time, I know he can.

I stayed up until two, last night, at a club.
My sole chance to see my brother twirl his ebony disks,
head bobbing, hands flying, the inch-long ash clinging
to the forgotten cigarette in his mouth.
A handsome man sat down next to me, and I searched for
    my brother
to interfere, like he always does, and spoil my night,
but he was at his turntables. Busy.

I smoked a begged cigarette last night. My brother's.
He shook his head and flicked his lighter.
Said, "You'll have to make your own mistakes, sis,"
as I watched my cigarette smoke rise, combine with his,
and dissipate.

Sarah Miller

Cadenza

At Birth

When I was born, there was great excitement and joy.
An eight-pound boy had emerged from his mother's womb.
I was crying and throwing a fit—
all the while I was covered with blood.
I had done something to hurt my mother—
I didn't mean to do it.
My broad shoulders had done the damage
and it was too late.
A father nowhere to be found—trucking somewhere.
A grandmother finally able to get over her prejudices
and come see her second grandchild.
An aunt thoughtful and caring, right there for comfort.
A big sister crawling somewhere around Vanderbilt.
A mother slowly getting rid of the pain.
A doctor happy it was finally over.
I was out and I could show the world what I could do.
My mother was full of love and happiness.

Andrew Lytle

Shield

You stand, shoulders hunched in like a turtle in its shell,
Your little belly engulfed in an oversized t-shirt
With holes in it from years of wear, not wanting to change.
You wear it often, whenever you think others will not see.
It is black, like the depth of your thoughts,
And thin like your outer shell that I finally broke through.

I can imagine when it was new,
You probably wore it everyday, a shield from judgment
That you could not peel off, even for your mother to wash
Because that would make it new again, one more smell to
    get used to.

I see it less often now, except when you want to prove that
    you are the same
But I see it in your eyes - joy that you blocked out for so
    long,
It seeps in through the holes in your tired garment,
And startles you.
Though it may eat through your comfort shirt like hungry
    moths,
It is okay to welcome happiness.

Jennifer Kiilerich

Cadenza

Good Googily Moogily Jesus, That's A Nice Hat

Jesus in a
       purple
and   gold
     velvet
       hat.
He had hat hair
       and a hangnail.
He sang
    a song
    about his hat:
                "I have a hat. It is purple. I have a hat. Tra la la. I eat pie. While I wear my hat. I lost my hat and I cried. Tra la la la la. I ate some more pie. I found my hat and I said "whoopee!" Tra la la laaaa laaaa. I have a hat."
This is why Jesus is known as
         a preacher, a son of God
        and   not
            a   songwriter.
But, bless him, he did try.

Melissa Bullock

Innocent Me
—inspired by Balthus' painting, *La Jupe Blanche*

In a world full of dark, stained evils,
I wear the white skirt,
the thread of innocence,
blinding light to my subconscious thoughts.
The trials of the world tire me easily.
It's hard to remain clean when temptation
seeps under the door,
running closer to me,
losing inky color in the cracks
of the wooden floor.

I lift my skirt gently, and fold it
in my lap, the hem slightly stained
with human desire.
No worry, Mother will bleach it out.
"You're a good girl," she smiles at me
while she scrubs the stain white.
She shuts the door behind her,
protects me from the world.

It's Saturday night again.
I sigh and read a book.
My body slouches, and my eyes
fix on an invisible object.
The white skirt grows heavy in
the night, its glow keeps me awake.
In desperation, I tear it to shreds,
play with the scraps on the floor,
enjoy my half-naked time.
Tomorrow will bring another
white skirt, draped neatly on
the ottoman beside my bed.

Gina Vizvary

Cadenza

Roger

There is this old man that lives with my mother and me. He is an enigma to me. I don't really know why he doesn't live by himself. That is what he cares about. He pays rent, though. I don't know how old he really is. Probably about fifty. I guess because he has the same wrinkles as my mother. He comes in late from work, goes back to his room and works till bed. Locked behind his fortress of papers. We keep our distance. We say hello as we pass, not making eye contact. That is about it. Roger, that's his name. He has lived with us for a while. He keeps to himself. He eats by himself. He sits by himself. Every once and a while he will come into my room and ask me how I am doing or some other flat question. Paying his dues, I suppose.

He is a ghost. A pillaging ghost. At night our house gets very still and dark. I fall asleep to the sound of the wind wrapping our house. Some nights there is no wind, and I hear silence as I go to bed. After a few seconds I begin to hear his typewriter pecking away, and it keeps me up. He finally stops. With a smile I shut my eyes to the peace, but it is fleeting. I first hear it in the hall and try to ignore it. It moves to my door. I try to wait it out. It moves into my room and I know it will stay the night, again. His ripping snore soon runs through the house, robbing every corner of its silence. His irregular pattern keeps me up for hours. I long for the nights with the wind.

He really doesn't pay enough rent. He eats my mother's food. She does his laundry for him. He really does nothing for the house. I suppose that is all right; he pays what he and my mother agreed to. Yeah, Roger keeps to himself, looks out for his face.

Sometimes my mother and I will be alone, watching TV together. He walks in. Over to my mother. He leans down and kisses her, and sometimes he throws in a phrase like, "I love you." Why the hell are you kissing my mother? Why doesn't she stop you? You just live here. Sometimes he would come in late from work. He would ask how my mother was and kiss her. Then he would leave her alone to go to the kitchen and eat the food she made, and she would watch him eat it. I don't know why he doesn't live by himself.

When the sounds of my tears crawl through the corridors of our old house, he continues his work, just as if he were in his own apartment. Just working for his school, tapping away. Sometimes I will be working late at night. I will hear his broken body lumber through the house for a midnight snack. My mind can map his route from the sounds. He is going to my mother's room, why? He only lives here.

My father died when I was very young. There is a man that has lived with my mother and me since then. His name is Roger. He keeps to himself and his work.

Shaffer Grubb

possum

he's coming in again like red
spread toes and bangs
straining my bloodshot watered eyes
while i wrestle with sleep
and lose
hand on my face
hair
kitten lips on my eyes
close
flutter
close
he says i love you
when he thinks i can't hear
i smile under my teeth
and let him think that
i am deaf

Ciciley Hoffman

Cadenza

Amanda

Amanda is home for the summer
He used to say she was an angel with her blue-gray eyes
She hates to be looked at
Staring out her bedroom window, facing east
She knows the ocean is there but does not see it—she hasn't
 seen it in years

She thinks of him
How he always let her stay up to watch TV
And helped with her homework
And taught her how to ride a bike and how to make the
 perfect tuna sandwich
And always kissed her and her bear goodnight

She looks at the photograph in her hand
The last time they were together
She had sand in her hair and a sunburn under her eyes
He had on a Hawaiian shirt and a straw hat
He was already becoming thin

She gets the bear from her closet
Its pink fur faded from years of being clutched and sobbed on
 and puked on and laughed with
She still doesn't understand why her mother tried to throw it
 out after he died
Why she couldn't take it to the funeral
And jump into the ground with her father, and get a second
 chance at the ocean.

Amy Lincoln

Manifesto of What the World Owes Me, Dammit

I wish I could live without a past
Without other people, because
they bring with them problems
And through sympathy I drown

I wish I could live without shame
It seems a useless emotion, and it
destroys our past. It makes memories of
Pain and happiness seem fleeting.

I wish I could live in poverty,
and think it the thing of kings,
when in fact, it is the refuge of
paupers and the toil of saints.

I wish I could live day to day,
and treat eating and sleeping
as a virtue, instead of gluttony
and sloth, and sins too numerable to name.

I wish I could not even wonder
who I was. To not have a spirit
crisis, to exist weightless, to have
no problems with conformity, with
comparison to peers and martyrs.

I wish I could live in bliss, or
failing that,
live in ignorance that life could be better.

Kirk Alexander

Cadenza

Another Quiet War
(On "Constellations," a series of paintings by Joan Miro)

Stiff rugged edges of a lifeless canvas
Attempt to bind the life of Joan Miro's creation
Within the frigid walls of scabby fabric.
They press from north and south, east and west,
Pursue amorphous shapes and bow-like stars
Into submission to the artist's pleasure.
As space itself succumbs to human hand,
Recedes before its self-assured brushstrokes,
Line wraps the color, fences it with darkness.
Eleven scarlet suns rise shyly—
Long subdued by chaos,
Amidst the rubble of demolished form.

Miro—you painted the serenity of coastal skies in 1941,
As Spain was bathed in blood and torn by struggle.
And peace is lacking yet in the colliding spheres,
And a single eye
That stares accusingly at me.

Lina Kharats

Sad but True

Though his hair will not twirl about my fingers
In golden ringlets
Or smell like the freshest spring breeze,
Though his figure will not ripple with
Lean muscle
Or be stronger than Ali Baba's forty thieves,
I will love him.

He will make obscene smells and noises
And sprout prickles in the morning.
Forget to say the right thing and lie,
And of course he will be boring.
But I will forgive him.

Lounging in his boxers,
He'll feel free to relieve his itches.
He will grunt and snore all through the night
Until I want to hit him.
But I will not.

For though he is not perfect,
And we know all men are not,
He is my double heartbeat
Or at least that's what I thought.

Missie Tidwell

Cadenza

Perchance a Fallacy

I didn't want to touch the doorknob, but when I did, it wasn't as cold as I had first imagined. It just seemed that, as my grandmother grew cold, so should her house emit a final, frigid emptiness. Once, Gramma said to me, "Listen: a lot of people are gonna give you shit in this life, and the more you take, the quicker your coffin gets nailed."

I was angry, then, remembering. Apparently, Gramma had equated "shit" with medicine, because I found boxes of it, once, untouched, in her closet. When confronted, she said that she was just tired, had eaten bacon everyday of her life, drank vodka straight, smoked oppressive cigars that billowed clouds of angry black smoke, and for what? "I was never meant to be this old, lovey," she muttered on her deathbed (an orthopedic monstrosity which boasted "hospital comfort in your home"), "I never should have outlived the sailors."

"Abbe! Oh, there you are. Help me with the chairs." My mother had arrived, jerking me from my memories.

"And put out the pie." How quaint this custom of the post-funeral feast, stuffing oneself, gorging on life-giving matter to have it all now, consuming. Glutting on life in case of death. I watched the stream of food and pitying, black-clad elders flow into her house, Gramma's ex-lovers, her sister, Peg (who could well have been my mother's birth mother considering her obsession with "fluffy kitties" and the Lord, our Savior Jesus Christ), some members of her church, her sewing circle. To this day, I cannot believe that Gramma belonged to something so bourgeois as a sewing circle, although Defeated, Wisconsin was certainly the perfect home for such "normalcy."

Rosalyn Black had been a "loose" woman, who bought pots of rouge by the case, played poker like a man, and was despised by respectable wives everywhere. She had discarded more lovers in a week than I would know in a lifetime, surely, and would leave my mother, that cat, a large inheritance composed of their monetary gifts. Rosalyn had associated with gangsters, had even hinted, once or twice, that her daughter had sprung from the loins of some criminal mastermind.

"Stop daydreaming! Sometimes you are positively worthless, Abbe. You take after Rosie," my mother spit through her thin lips.

Somehow, my mother could even make a word signifying my beloved Gramma sound hateful. She obviously envied her mother her glamour. My mother wore pantsuits and buns, and her red lipstick inevitably ended up on her teeth and the wrinkles surrounding her mouth more often than on her lips. She was fussy and fastidious, making it hard to imagine her childhood. My grandmother, however, must have led the most fanciful and fulfilling childhood possible. She had poems from ardent lovers in her closet with dried roses pressed between them, completed by one tragic farewell letter with no return address. I found them once. They were mysterious and exciting, with tragic references to her "affliction" in them. I had often longed to have the same romantic "affliction."

She softened. "I know you're upset, honey." I tried to smile up at her, marveling at the difficulty with which she forced out the term of endearment. "We all are, but Grandma has gone to a better place." I nodded, picturing a homicidal snake wrapping around her bony throat.

"Let's go inside. Huh, kiddo?" A cynical college student, incidentally, should not be called "kiddo."

"'Kay, Mom." Of course, I shouldn't allow it, either. We entered the house, being careful not to touch.

I stood in a corner of the house, being condoled. Hard to imagine that this was the same house in which I had read musty, romantic books with my grandmother, sipping brandy. They were still wary with me after my performance at the funeral, but I fulfilled my duty.

"She would have appreciated your presence here," I repeated, mechanically, like the proverbial broken record, to the faceless masses. That was bullshit; she didn't care about these people, no more than they cared about her. All of them had ignored her when she got sick. They didn't want to see her vivacity fade, to remind them that they were fossils, no longer needed

Cadenza

by mainstream society. They were selfish old relics, and, with Gramma's presence out of their lives, they would be reduced to watching game shows with their cats.

"Don't call me Grandma! I'm not some old crow who wears adult diapers and underwear that comes up to my tits!" She was there, in my head. In the room. I reeled around, her raspy voice echoing in my ears. Everyone was staring.

"Where is she?" I howled, and stumbled into the garden to vomit. The guests soon left, despite my mother's assertions that I "will be fine. She's just a little tired. Don't go."

They must have thought I was nuts. Especially after my eulogy.

I sat politely, erect with my hands folded into my lap. Every few minutes, a wrinkled face swiveled in my direction. The looks seemed more curious than a mere mourning granddaughter would warrant. I could have cared less.

I had a piece of notebook paper in my lap, complete with an approved speech my mother had written about my personal feelings towards my grandmother. When the preacher finished his standard eulogy about a nondescript person with my grandmother's name (I imagined that he had a file saved in his computer with this very general speech intact, save for a space for each individual's name to be penciled in.), I rose and walked to the podium. Whispers followed me, stopping short as I turned to face them.

"Gramma..." I started. I felt weak. My calves turned to mush. Eyes bored into me. "Was a compassionate and loveable woman." My remorse transformed itself in an instant. Rage seeped behind my eyes, gritted my teeth. Fury clenched and unclenched my fists, slowly. How dare they even presume to think that their presence was required?! Or helpful? Or anything but a slap in the face to the only person in the whole damn church who really knew her? I impulsively changed my approach. "Gramma was one righteous bitch," was as far as I got before my mother gasped and escorted me hurriedly from the church.

"Have you no respect?" she demanded, tears dripping from her squinty eyes. "You are so ungrateful; you're grandmother would be ashamed..."

Cadenza

"Bullshit!" I screamed in a louder voice than intended. "This is all for you. This is your asinine way of 'doing your duty.' You just want to appear to be a considerate daughter. Well, you weren't, so why not drop the act! You begrudged that woman her every achievement, not to mention every visit you contributed to her hospital stay." I was stopped then by an abrupt and wholly unexpected slap from my mother. I wouldn't have thought her capable of such an impassioned act.

My great-aunt Peg stayed with us that night. She came up to see me when I recovered from my delirium, and brought me soup. I had refused my mother's previous offer of nourishment, in the form of a pimento cheese sandwich with the crusts cut off. That was my mother's idea of home cooking, and the surest way to affect her was to refuse it. Peg could care less.

"Are you okay?" she asked in a cold tone.

"Fine, thank you." I could be distant, too.

"I know you think you know everything, after being in that elitist college atmosphere, but you're wrong," she suddenly burst.

"I know. Wisdom comes with age, and, as long as you have your own teeth and hair, you possess only the most superficial of knowledge," I retorted. I had really come full circle this trip. The mild-mannered apathist had suddenly transformed into an emotional volcano spewing hurtful, intended lava.

"There are no absolutes in this life, Abbe," she said softly, staring into my eyes. "Your mother is not a shallow, selfish villain and my sister was never a romantic martyr. Sometimes I think Rosie expected her daughter to emerge as a miniature adult, responsible for herself. Your mother wasn't exactly expected."

"So Mom had to grow up with a private tutor, jetting around Europe. My heart aches with pity for the poor creature."

"You should talk to her about this, but... did you know your mother miscarried?"

I got the impression from the tone of her voice that she had been prepared to utter another revelation altogether.

"No. When?"

"Before you were born. I— you should talk to her." This disdainful old woman seemed to be almost frightened.

"Fine. Send her up," I returned, yawning in a transparent attempt to be nonchalant about this scandalous illumination of my mother.

"Perhaps I will," she demurred, suddenly very conscious of the gloves in her lap. She rose. "You two should discuss this."

My mind raced. How could a timid creature like my mother ever have tested the overbearing morality of a 1950s society by allowing herself to become pregnant? Had the father been the same man as my father?

"Wait, Peg. Was he my...mine?" My voice jettisoned up to squeaky, unsure heights that I had no idea it could reach.

"He was your father, yes," she said, crisply. "Thankfully, you didn't inherit much from him." Then, remembering her propriety, "I'll send up Mona."

I wanted to grab her and force her back into her chair. I wanted to demand answers. This was the first human-seeming thing I'd heard about my father. Suddenly, he was three-dimensional, and my source was snapped away from me. Where would she have even met a boy? She had toured Europe with my grandmother until she reached adulthood, and the people my grandmother associated with would not have had children. At least, not "respectable" children. Maybe my father wasn't the admirable Vietnam casualty Mom always made him out to be.

What a scandal it must have been. Gramma would have been enraged, and possibly even kicked Mom out. After all, she may not have been conventional, but she would still want to maintain some semblance of morality in her reputation. Perhaps that's why we all now lived in the most depressingly cheerful midwestern town in America. Hell, Gramma could have caused the miscarriage in a drunken rage one night, for all I knew; I was almost elated that my family should have been so unconventional.

But then I stopped supposing. A picture formed, in my mind, of a girl three years my junior in a strange country. She is pregnant, bent from the effort of carrying a baby on her small, semi-formed frame. She is not allowed out lest her condition be surmised by the gossiping populous of the intrusive town. Her head is slumped with shame as her mother berates her for being lustful and for being so damned much trouble. She tries desperately to help her mother, to right the injustice she has done.

After being forced into the role of wife, this is where mother must have learned the art of tidiness. God knows Gramma would never have had interest enough to show her, if she even knew herself. The girl in my mind weeps, quietly, and tends to the chores she has to do because no one else will, tears mixing with the gray dishwater infested with leftovers from a burnt dinner. She will wail when she realizes the life inside her is gone, imagining, possibly, that she was to blame. I felt tears wet on my own cheeks as my mother entered the room, solemnly.

"Peg said you wanted me, honey; is there anything I can do for you?"

I hugged her fiercely, then, gripping her to me as if I could erase years of anguish with one embrace. "Why didn't you tell me, Mom?"

"What?" she asked, taken aback but obviously pleased by my unexpected affection.

"About the miscarriage," I whispered, gently as if the word itself could harm her.

"What?!" she exclaimed. "Oh, you've been listening to Aunt Peg, haven't you?" she says smoothly, rising. "She has been under tremendous stress, and her mind is going. You must know that." She busies herself cleaning my immaculate room. "Don't let her imaginings worry you. Is that all you needed, honey?"

I paused, studying her. "No, mama. Could you bring me a sandwich? Please?"

My mother smiled; she loves to caretake. "Well, of course."

We haven't spoken about it since. I still have a lot of unanswered questions about my father. I wonder if he ever cooked for my mom. I wonder if he or my grandmother wiped her tears after the miscarriage. I hope someone did.

Sarah Miller

Cadenza

The Temptress Smell

Smells intermingle like a set of watercolors left in the rain,
Spreading and dispersing to saturate the air;
Dancing around street corners like a sleek cat,
Provoking noses with its sly meow.
Smell is a temptress when
There is bread baking in the oven,
Wanting only hunger in return.
Smell anticipates you,
Waiting to conquer like Genghis Khan
When the trash can lid is removed.
Wet clothes slap around the cave of the dryer,
And smell lumbers out like a friendly bear.
It collects like dust and multiplies like rabbits,
While smiling an invisible Cheshire grin,
To aggravate and delight.

Aliene Howell

Night

It feels cool
and provokes a slight shiver,
like a ghost,
my father perhaps,
passing through my soul.
It was night
when he walked out the door
and didn't look back.
He returns when I close my eyes
and turn out the light.

I hear the breeze
whispering in my ear,
singing a silent tune.
I hear the mystery
beckoning me,
telling me not to be afraid.
I feel its arms pulling me in,
Its fingers gripping tightly.
I can taste
the sweetness of despair,
and feel
the comfort of loneliness.
I see night
When I close my eyes.
It's looking back at me,
Calling me.
Pleading with me to come in.

Te'Meka Roberts

Cadenza

Awakening

Mom's voice sings
above the vacuum cleaner,
shrill and strong.
She's holding onto something.
I sit at the glass table
and sip mint tea,
swallowing the tension.
Dad walks in,
placing persimmons
on the transparent surface.
"The park is just
beautiful right now."
I nod. It always is.
Mom stands in the doorway.
"Good morning,"
in a honey disguise,
that drips from the bottle
and dissolves
in the faint brown liquid,
glaring at him
from across the room.
They begin to throw words,
but I've already slipped out,
escaped to the new day,
barefoot on gravel.
My cat meows
with questioning eyes
and rubs soft fur
against my ankles.
The brick house fades
against the brightness
of the maples.

Cadenza

I look up and smile
at a curious bluebird,
perched on the gutter,
twitching its tail.
With sudden precision,
it plunges upward
and flies into the sky
leaving only a fluttering memory.
The day lifts
and pushes me towards its flight.
I turn from the sun
and begin to follow my shadow,
wondering where
the light will lead.

Alisa Loveman

Dreaming in the Hallway

A bright dream of mountains
comes into focus.
The sun gleams off the spray
of water crushing limestone.
The sun filters through the tall oaks,
contrasting shadow and light on the riverbank.
The light bends and reflects
as a vortex forms around my paddle.
A light switch destroys my vision
as my pupils contract in the light.
Footsteps and voices
walk across the stained oak floors,
slamming lockers in frustration.
Shadows are cast upon the books in my bag
as I reach for my pen.

Chris Michie

Cadenza

Jesica

Demon shadow puppets,
Dobermans and bunnies,
hurl obscenities from the walls.
"People tell me what to say."
They bite off the heads of stuffed animals,
Yoda and Papa Smurf sit blindly before the silhouettes.
There's a silkscreen in the corner,
Warhol-induced t-shirts lie on the carpet,
Brillo pads and Campbell's soup.
She wore pink cardigans
reeking of smoke,
the warehouse scent of Southern Thrift.
We sat in swings at night
hating our best friends.
A kitten with blue fur comes roaring up,
jumping into her lap.
Her own blue locks drape over its devil-tipped ears,
looking like an angel.
Unfeminine in a babydoll dress,
Camel unfiltered pursed between her lips,
squishing mud between her pink toenails,
holding a jar of sour cream,
she used to eat it on everything.

Brandy Ratcliff

Cadenza

For Grandmother

Life is only a passing moment;
time, the cold hand
stealing the seconds that slowly swallow
your husband,
your sister,
your life.
And so you clean out the attic,
give away pictures and objects
that can no longer bring you as much joy
as a phone call from your children
who no longer bring their families at Christmas.
Memories slip through your fingers
like fistfuls of sand.
And the tighter you cling to them
with your wrinkled hands,
the faster they go,
scattering in the wind
and taking with them
a part of you.
You sit hollow and alone
in a large empty house,
waiting for death to come
and keep you company.

Aisha Siebert

Cadenza

A Quiet Evening at Home

He was not one of those guys. He was not like them; he hated guys like that. But it had happened. So fast. Calling it fast doesn't even fit; it had almost happened backwards.

She was in the dining room with her best friend. "Has he ever done this before?" His wife gave off an answer muffled by her tears. All the candles lit with a yellow pallor. Allied against him. He sat in the dark blue living room from which he could hear their conversation. Their voices glided across the entryway in front of the stairs and into his head. "You know what you have to do." He sat in the darkness with his leg shaking and his head tilted toward the floor. The room blue, soaked with night. The only light from the yellow candles that reflected in from the dining room. He could see nothing; there was nothing to point at. He could only sit in the darkness. So quick he could barely remember. His arm lifted his trembling hand to his face. He could only make out the silhouette. "Why did he do it?" Her response was too weak to reach his ear. He got up and paced. His feet were not able to cross the entryway. That yellow light. He heard them continue. The room got darker, bluer. He wasn't one of those guys. He felt his hand. His ring made an impression on the top side of his finger from the impact. He went back and collapsed on his couch and stared at the ceiling, only a few feet up. There was nothing to do in this dark room but wait. Nothing to blame. No way to justify. He could only sit here, wasting time, hanging on that blank yellow light with his dark blue hands. He listened to them throughout the evening. "You should come stay with me tonight," the friend proposed. Time passed. "We should call the police." The yellow light retreated as the candles went out one by one in the dining room. His wife and her partner didn't seem to notice. He stood up and went to the door, left, and walked down the front steps. He took a right at the bend in the sidewalk and observed them through the window. Her hands supported her head, and her friend's hand was rubbing her back.

Cadenza

The yellow candles lit their faces from all angles. The shadows shimmered.

He got into his car and turned it on. He pulled out and crept down the blue, moonlit road. No, not his bar tonight. He wasn't facing that. "It will never happen again, I promise." He drove and found another bar. After going in and sitting at the bar, it didn't take long for him to notice that everyone was speaking Spanish. The dry impact of his knuckle on her cheekbone resonated in his head. Rewind, play. He ordered his beer in English; it sufficed. He noticed a man in the corner carrying the crowd. He had never noticed how inconsequential everything sounds in Spanish, when you don't know a lick of it. He kept hearing that impact. "He promised it would never happen again, he promised." As he finished his drink, he stared at the beer that had settled on the bottom, run down from the sides. He wasn't one of those guys, nope. He would try to drink this last bit, but most of it would gather on the sides before it reached his mouth. She couldn't stop crying. He finally put his money on the bar and left. His new friends took little notice. He took the blue road back. The moon in the western sky was yellow, a brilliant yellow.

He cut his lights as he entered the driveway; his wife's friend's car was gone. Feeling his way, he went around to the back of the house via the driveway, then through the back entrance. He paused as he entered the kitchen. Sometime in the eternity of night the last candles were extinguished, and the blue blackness devoured the house. A patch of the streetlight crossed her face. The only light. Her fingers tenderly touched the wound. He went in and sat down at the kitchen table across from her. They sat in silence. "I don't know why this happened," she said. After a pause he began to speak, but she cut him off, "But it doesn't matter now, we are way past that…. We can't go back to where we were," she said. They sat with the table between them. Time passed; neither had any sense of how long it was. Her eyes locked onto the dark, with her finger rested on the wound. He fidgeted quietly with a paper napkin. Folding it. Tearing it. Unfolding it. It was almost black, the only light reflecting from the street off her cheek. His look was not fixed like hers. He examined the napkin, he looked out the window. Back to the napkin.

The entire episode played in his head as he sat there. It had happened so fast. He had come home from work. "Fix the shed."

"Not right now."

"Well, it's been 'not right now' for about three weeks. When is it going to happen?"

"I had a bad day. Not right now." They continued for twenty minutes, increasing in volume and stubbornness. "You aren't hearing me," he said.

"I hear you fine, but the shed needs to be fixed, today, now."

"You aren't listening." He watched it happen. He watched his body do his bidding. His fist drove through her cheek from the side. She heard through her bones. Her eyes were closed, but she saw it flare in technicolor. Later she couldn't recall how it felt, just the thought of how it felt. He froze, and stared at where it had happened. They were in the living room. She went broken to the dining room. The friend called, then came. Her tears filled the air.

His mind returned to the present. "I don't know how to fix this. All I know is I would do anything I could to go back and change things."

"There are different paths for us now, not all of them bad, nor good," she said.

"But none lead back to where we were," he said

Every few minutes he would raise his head and look over to her. Hoping. She never looked back, just fixed on that void. He finally put the shredded napkin on the table and stood. He walked around the table and stopped behind her. He placed his limp hand on her shoulder. He felt his fingertips spread over her silk blouse. She hadn't changed clothes since he got home that afternoon. She felt warm through the cloth. He could faintly feel her heart beat. She didn't turn away from his hand and she didn't reach for it. She sat there staring, like a porcelain doll. He bit his lower lip and slightly nodded. His hand slid

Cadenza

off her shoulder, and he went through the dining room and up the stairs. He couldn't even see the shadows in the darkness. Blue turned to black. But there was one square of light from the street. It stretched across the dining room as he left it. He went up the stairs, feeling his way.

Shaffer Grubb

Using Everything

The plains Indians
used every part of the buffalo:
Meat for nourishment,
Hide for clothing,
Bones for tools.

My grandfather was the same.
A carpenter by trade,
Every piece of board was used,
No nail was wasted.

He learned to use
everything in the '40s
in a prison camp
in eastern Germany.
Anything edible was consumed
by those dead men.

A guard once sicced
his German Shepherd
on my grandfather's barracks.
Meat for nourishment,
Hide for food,
All they threw out:
Dead dog bones.

John Stringham

Cadenza

What Mother Says

Don't open the door to strangers,
lock your doors when driving,
that's what mother always says.
Never trust people you don't know
and don't talk to strangers
is what mother says.
But why should I be scared of strange people or homeless people?
Why doesn't she tell me to look out
for the man in the three-piece suit?
He doesn't have to steal my car
because he's robbing me on the insurance.
He doesn't have to jump me or beat me up
because he's making a killing off the hospital bill,
when I fall and break my ankle
because I'm trying to run, but look like I'm walking while
    looking over my shoulder
because there are some suspicious-looking street thugs behind me.
The guys at the homeless shelter
only want a few dollars of my money
whereas the people mother looks at and says,
"You should be like that man when you get older!",
are trying to take every penny I have.
What mother says.... Hmmph, go figure.

Marchello Gray

Lauren

She is sprawled on the couch
Cheap alcohol flowing through her body.
Her head hangs off the end.
She is pretending to be dead.
Thinking she's asleep,
the other girls and I leave her
go into another room
so she can have peace.
Later she appears in our doorway
like a wild-eyed Medusa
dark hair tumbling around her face.
Her thin body is unsteady
Silver flashes from her wrists and fingers
as she points at us
Accusing.
"I was dead," she spits.
"I was dead and waiting to see
if you noticed.
You don't care."
And her fragile form collapses
in a bony heap.
We go to her, pick her up
lay her down on the bed.
She mumbles and cries;
her life, her parents, her looks—
Why does the world not pity her?
Not fall down in sorrow
At the burdens she bears?
We soothe and stroke her
silently
Knowing she hears only herself.

Abbe Rose Kopra

Cadenza

Final Concert
From a painting by Henri Matisse: *Woman with Violin*

Peacock eyes stare straight
And light dances behind her.
She faces the dark and yawns,
Propping her heavy head with her fist.

Her sighs rattle the table legs
And the rosin in her violin case.
Her bow nearly drops to the floor.

Her shoulders and feet melt into the
Crimson carpet woven haphazardly by
Fingers that only know how
To trill, to glissando, to arpeggio.

Darkness shrivels under her eyes
As she struggles again to escape
The stage lights that reveal everything—
The starkness of undeserved fame.

Christine Lee

Fallen Angel

You gave me angel wings.
Slowly, stealthily,
You wrapped feathery bonds around my heart.
Extolling my beauty.
One layer.
My purity.
That's two.
My softness, my abundance of love.
Somehow I didn't hear the lock click.

And now I struggle.
I can't breathe.
I look to you with panicked eyes,
you who loves me so.

Smiling calmly, you come at me
and wrap me in your arms
tightly.

Desperate
I try to scream
No sound comes out
Because you're pressing my face into your chest.

I love you, I love you, I love you,
you croon.
And I've lost the strength
to break free.

You smile again
Open the door to your pride
And place my lifeless body
On the top shelf.

Abbe Rose Kopra

Cadenza

Temptation

I sit too long and the walls cave in.
I think of my thoughts and start to cry.
I sit alone in a pool of sin.

My tears fall like raindrops on tin.
Soon the weeping ceases and my face dries,
But I sit too long and the walls cave in.

I lift my head and the play begins—
I pray toward the white plaster sky.
I sit alone in a pool of sin.

I fight with these emotions at every turn.
Father, forgive me, but I am tired of lies.
I sit too long and the walls cave in.

A faithful servant I have not been,
And these feelings I cannot deny,
So I sit alone in a pool of sin.

These thoughts are a heavy burden.
Satan's clutches grow stronger with each lie.
I sit too long and the walls cave in.
I sit alone in a pool of sin.

Cle'shea Crain

Nightmares

I could have stopped you,
because I knew what was going to happen.
But I was afraid of you,
sitting with your back turned.
In a room filled with darkness and demons,
crying bloody tears with your hands
reaching out
to catch the lightning streaks,
and me
not strong enough for the both of us.
The note you left behind
has left enough guilt
to burn the inside of my body
like acid,
three times over, and in my dreams
I see your face,
the distorted vision, and those eyes.
Eyes that wake me
from my sleep in the middle
of the night. That thought
sits in the back of my mind.
And I wonder
what happened to you that night.

DeAndrea Witherspoon

Cadenza

"Girl Interrupted"
—*Seventeen* Magazine, September, 1999

...says the headline.
I am warm in bed
Tracing flowers on my quilt with my finger—
"Young girls are treated like slaves in Ghana."

I grip the magazine with white knuckles
clean from just being washed and
soft from lack of work.
A Pakistani woman gropes the air with red hands
As she dies slowly by a shot from her own brother.
An "honor killing," I read.

My mother comes to kiss me goodnight and
Wraps maternal arms around me.
In Ghana girls are torn away from nurturing mothers
to become servants to priests hungry for new flesh.
Trokoski, a traditional practice of degradation:
Girls must be cleansed of sins of their ancestors, they claim.

I run my hands through my blonde hair,
Still dripping from a hot shower.
A woman in Togo, Africa sits in her blood that falls in drops
From insides, ripped out by an untrained doctor.

I squeeze my mess of wet hair, letting water fall onto the
    yellow pillow
that I threw playfully at my sister yesterday.
A girl in Afghanistan will have her ankle cut off for trying
    to play.

I adjust my flannel boxers that are too short for me now,
But oh so comfy on cold nights, and even on warm ones.
When it is excruciatingly hot, the Afghani Taliban*
burdens females with monstrous cloaks,
Hardly an eyehole to see through,
No opening for the mouth to cry out—

I close the magazine and sip a glass of water,
Cool, calm, and refreshing as a cup of curdled milk.

Jennifer Kiilerich

*The Taliban is a strict government that took over Afghanistan and restricted women's most basic rights.

Rain vs. Skydivers

I bet the rain really hates skydivers. If the rain doesn't hate skydivers, it should at least be envious, because skydivers get to wear helmets and parachutes. A skydiver gets to enjoy the rush of falling towards the ground, while the rain just thinks, "When I land, my little melon head is going to ripple and fragment into a thousand pieces. My body will make a little bit of liquid shrapnel that will land on—and then be eaten by—some grass."

Skydivers should be envious of the rain, too, because rain falls so regularly. It would probably be fun to roll off a duck's back. The life of a raindrop actually seems kind of sweet, because you get yourself up and down, and there's no worrying about the skill of the pilot. Plus, I bet rain makes some funny faces when it starts evaporating in its descent.

I bet the moon looks at all of them and laughs, because it gets to be way high up and never fall.

Kirk Alexander

Cadenza

Kids

So young and innocent
Full of life and energy
Open-minded
Ready to learn
Easily influenced
Always watching you
Up to something
Outgoing and friendly
Hug their parents
Love to play
Say silly phrases
Say mean things
Want big dogs
Get dirty and sweaty
Hate baths at night
Enjoy the outdoors
Fear monsters
Watch cartoons
Go swimming
Welcome summer
Wait for Santa
Eat lots of junk
Despise vegetables
Our next generation
Free to explore and
Expand their minds
Need nurturing.
Succeed in life.

Andrew Lytle

Cadenza

Mother and Son in Mali
  A Photograph in *National Geographic*

Remnants of a lost Eden
 cake the sides of their faces.
 The hot midday sun glares down.
 They lie upon the earth that
 mothered them,
 enraptured by a moment of
 peaceful rest...

Until they are awakened
 by the howl of sharded sand
 piercing the wind;
the sound of the war
 their nurturer has waged against them.
 Indiscriminate in every sense
 except time and place.

The Past merges with the cries
 of how *their* land
 has disowned them
 and rises
 to a deafening wail.
While the desert
 sits silently
 unmoved
 unswayed.

Karen Tankersley

Cadenza

After Reading the Poem
"Concert in the Garden" by Octavio Paz

I, too, remember that concert.
Only, instead of a small garden scene,
it gathers an unusual crowd
in the bottom room of a pizzeria.
The cement floor swims with Birkenstocks,
Doc Martens, a few high heels,
and my bare feet.
Music brings them to step
around the maze of people,
and find a secluded corner.
Stems of metal and bone reach out
and blossom into dance.
People wander in and out,
from sound to silence,
silence to sound,
to catch a smoke or a friend
in transition,
and I wonder which came first.
Night drifts through me
like the ever-present river
that is the world.
Stepping outside, the still air
relieves me
from the noisy room,
but after a few moments,
I long to be back,
to take the current in my arms.

I realize that
silence follows sound
as sound follows silence,
until they lose distinction
and the concert winds them together
so that our feet disappear,
and I, too, walk lost between the worlds.

Alisa Loveman

The Willow Tree

The moon rises in the twilight.
I peer through the willows
that drape over the pond.
As the breeze gently ripples the water,
I feel its chill through the branches.
My eyes follow the wake
until they catch a glimpse of a swan.
Slowly gliding through the pond,
it creates a wake of its own.
The moon's reflection is distorted
by the swan's ripples as it swims by
The sweet smell of fresh air
blows through the willow branches
and into my face.
I smell the rain
approaching in the distance.
I look to the sky,
but the stars are still shining.
The swan continues to swim across the pond
until it is barely in view.
I lean back against the willow
and watch the ripples shimmer the moon's reflection.

Chris Michie

Cadenza

Grams and St. Jude

You had three boys,
Could whip any man at tennis
And knock back Crown Royal with Father Pete.
Lindied in New Broadway with Charlie Anacharico,
Took care of Nanny until the very end,
And still had time to cook meatballs
And dust behind beds.

Then your body attacked itself.
Legs started to go.
You were no longer my tennis coach.
You were no longer the family's strong arm.

Complications?
Wheelchair?
Depression. Mood-swings.
Hobble around on a cane,
Don't want to go out or see friends
Cursing. "I can do the damn dishes myself!"
Charlie lost his dance partner.
Hospital visits in the City,
Bruises from the falls.

You told me that you'd rather jump
off the Tappan-Zee in rush hour traffic.
Will you take your tired prayer books with you?
Will St. Jude be by your side, all the way down
to the Hudson?

Gina Vizvary

Reflection

I am the daughter of the eighteenth generation
Of the famous king who created the Korean language.
I would be a stricken princess with no freedom
If invasions had not crushed the empire.

Surrounded by heavenly beams of light
That create silhouettes of tired grandmothers
Who manage to stay awake during a sermon,
I fidget in my chair under the glowing presence of God.

My family is loud and overbearing.
Cousin after cousin comes to live in the room next to me,
Bothering me when I study, leaving me when I am alone.

The last drop of sun before darkness spreads through the sky.
I am the student, working to finish assignments and projects,
Half awake, dialing all my friends' numbers
Only to realize they are at work or at a soccer game.
Alone, I struggle through chemical formulas and explications.

I am the smile that greets you in the morning of the rainiest day,
That listens to everyone's inside jokes but understands none of them.
I am the silent one who cannot fully relate to the Civil Rights
    Movement—
A character of an unwritten story by Amy Tan.

I am the beginning of a set future,
A future with wide open doors and windows slightly ajar,
I will squeeze through those windows and leave doors open
To let hope shine on me in times of victory
To let hope lift me up when I stumble.

Christine Lee

Cadenza

Room 104

PUSH!
A new mother screams
in bittersweet agony
bursting with anxiety
ONCE MORE! HARDER!
first the head, then the shoulders
the little belly button, the tiny feet
a new life
IT'S A GIRL!
a princess
her first day of school
"mommy don't leave me"
I love you sweetheart
her first boyfriend
her first kiss
prom queen
high school graduate
...a woman president?
MRS. WALKER...SHE'S NOT BREATHING
the umbilical cord wraps tighter around the baby's neck
the doctors try to untangle her
a new life fades away
outside doctors rush up and down the halls
sirens can be heard in the distance
horns honk from traffic on the street below
the sounds of life can be heard everywhere
but silence fills Room 104.

Marchello Gray

That Was Then

Once a young boy,
he stood in front of the mirror.
Tears streamed down his face
and the saline made his busted lip sting like fire.
He stared at burns and bruises
caused by cigars and man-sized fists.
Bruises only a father could supply.
This boy, old enough to know that it's not right,
but too small and too scared to retaliate.

Once a problem teen,
he sat with friends in noisy hallways
wishing he had a cigarette,
wishing his mother hadn't died.
He smoked and drank for a release
from his life of guidance counselors and homework.
Too often he was found passed out in back alleys
and stoned out of his mind in classrooms:
head plastered to the desk, lips soaked in saliva.

Now older, wiser,
he tries to leave his past behind him
but the memories are overwhelming.
He recalls lying awake at night in the two-bedroom apartment,
waiting for Dad to come home drunk.
Fearfully anticipating him kicking in the door,
just for one punch
directed to an area that's already too sore to even touch.
With his own children, he promises himself,
he'll never let them know his kind of sadness.

Cle'shea Crain

Cadenza

Void of Dreams

The sound of the aging fan spinning rhythmically can be heard in the background. Katherine is chattering away, trying to conceal her fatigue, but she is interrupted by yawns. I pull back her covers; she arranges her stuffed animals, careful to make sure her ragged bunny is close. I bend to kiss her freckled nose and sweep her strawberry hair away from the delicate features of her face.

I turn to walk out her room and she asks, "What will my good dream be?"

I pause...trying to come up with the most correct image to give an eight-year-old child. But all my education has not prepared me to answer a question so simplistic. I look around the room trying to discern what she loves and would want to dream of. There's a poster she made for art class of a picnic—hot pink pieces of watermelon, fiery red ants, and a checkered blanket. Perhaps she would enjoy dreaming of skipping through a field of flowers where she can stay forever young....

But Katherine does not ponder ramifications of growing old; she does not fear losing her youth. I turn to her closet door where her backpack is hung. Papers are spilling out, and a social studies book peers behind a folder. Maybe Katherine should dream of being valedictorian of her graduating class....

But school is not about grades for Katherine. It's still a chance to be with playmates, to think boys are yucky, and to know that slumber parties are the best. I quickly turn, trying to find something that will spark my imagination to give Katherine her happy dream. I see her gymnastics outfit lying on the floor. What could be happier than winning an Olympic gold medal?

And yet, winning is of no importance to Katherine's untainted mind. What happy dream can I give her? How can I tell her she lives the best dream of all, of having a life with small fears, no knowledge of failure.

Some would say experience helps you attain dreams. But my experience leaves me faltering, incapable of putting a pleasant image into a child's mind. Experience, maturation—they have ruined my ability to dream, for I cannot give Katherine a happy dream tonight.

    I sit down on her bed, wrap my arms around her, and tell her she is my happy dream. I wait until her breath is slow, steady, like the spinning of the fan. I turn as I pass through the door to catch a glimpse of her serenity. I breathe in the smells of childhood, wishing life was as easy as believing in fairies.

Christen Sewell

Beneath Anger

Vacant eyes bear down,
    having nowhere else to gaze.
A mouth curls into a twisted grin.
Piercing cries fall on deaf ears.
The dark trees stand witness
    to mock you.
The soft moon cannot
    penetrate their canopy.
As your body is vandalized,
    the rough edges of dirt scratch
    your exposed skin.
A violent shock spreads
    and you can almost hear
    the sound of fragile tissue ripping.

A few moments are the ghosts
    that haunt you years after.
Sitting on a black leather couch
    in front of an Armani suit
    that asks where your anger formed.

Somewhere between no and a gun.

Karen Tankersley

Cadenza

Canoe Trip

Barely able to reach
over the gunwales,
I stick my fingers
in the paddle-formed vortex
as they swirl by
with every mastered stroke.
My little fingers make wakes
as the canoe glides through the water.

Looking around, the mountains
stretch the limits of the sky,
towering over me in the canoe.
The world is so big.

The water chills my fingers
as the drops of the river
fall back to their home,
one by one.

Fog fades away
as the sun climbs into the sky.
Looking ahead, the water
wraps around the limestone
forming an eddy,
a serene refuge
from the torrent ahead.
I grip the thwart
and brace.

Chris Michie

No, I Didn't Go to School Today

There was a tiny trickle of blue
running beneath the gnarled oaks.
I sat in one and fell,
adding salt tears to the stream.

I peeled a rose from its sleepy bed,
I smelled it, laughing.
I tore the petals away,
the leaves, the roots,
throwing it, with desperation—
a childhood tantrum.

I stared all day,
the open wound dripping
scarlet in my socks.
He can't see anymore,
the reaper sewed his eyes shut.

I'm only lying here so still,
my energy is spent.
I already ripped the walls with my tiny fingers,
flinging dressers and TVs,
singeing the carpet with matches,
turning my bed into the flames.

I wanted to be beautiful like the roses,
untouched, not torn by a heartbroken child,
but in the dirt.

Now it smells like tire rubber
in my twin bed,
as I lie scratching the scab on my knee,
shards of grass sticking out.

Brandy Ratcliff

Cadenza

Last Days

I sat up late last Saturday night,
thinking.
Staring at the hospital bed.
Seeing you lying there as pain crept through your body.
There was something I wanted to say,
but I was saving it for years down the road.
And then it hit me,
Like lightning out of the sky.
What if that day was never to come,
and the words never crossed my lips.
What if you never knew how I truly felt,
The way I admire everything about you.
The way I fall to my knees at night,
teary-eyed, giving thanks for you.

I had always let you believe
that I didn't care,
but it was all a lie.
A lie born in my heart,
to protect my soul.
Then I realized that without you knowing,
my efforts were lost.
If the world ever falls from the sky,
or blackens over,
Know that I'll be here to support you,
or light your way.

Cadenza

As we approach the last days,
I breathe easily,
Knowing that I've said
All that needed to be said.
No more secrets
Hidden in closets
locked by pain
and fear.
Sickness has taken over your body,
Nothing can be changed.

Can what I feel
Hurt so bad that it would
break the walls that surround me?
If my lips never part again,
know from my eyes:
I cherish these last days.

Te'Meka Roberts

Cadenza

Courtney

Crying, she came to me.
Said she couldn't take it anymore.
Got a job and school...and her
baby takes a lot of energy.

Wish she had a father, she says.

He left before Katelyn was born.
Said it wasn't his.
Already has two, can't take more.

Mom wants me to get a second job.

Her mom hates her,
an unrelenting hate. Wants to take her baby
and kick her out of the house.
It's not right.

She is rocking now with her knees
locked within her arms.
Sobbing.

How'm I going to be a good mother?
I'm a child, but I can't be.

The good ole days, she says,
I'm too young to have good ole days.
I just want to take my child and go.

She has a hard time in school.
Friends are junkies, just got suspended
for fighting, might get kicked out.

Cadenza

*What am I going to do? I just want
to take my child and go.*

Over and over again.
Mascara is running down her face
from her red eyes.

Katelyn crawls towards a socket
in the wall.
Courtney mindlessly covers it
with her hand while continuing to talk.
Good mother.

Take me away from here, I can't stay,
she says, barely over a whisper.

Missie Tidwell

Jane

Jane sits in a dark room
in a stone house on Coolidge Avenue.
The rain inside her paints the world black.
The sweetly poisonous memory
of her father's trembling hands
leaves a stamp like fingerprints in dust.
She watches the summer heat rise
through the attic window
The ivy covering the outside wall
slowly chokes the house.
The ocean throws itself at her
as it explodes and sinks
And she doesn't blink.

Amy Lincoln

Cadenza

New Light

I was born March 10, 1982
at Vanderbilt Hospital in Nashville, Tennessee.
I had a white mother and a black father.
I was mixed—this only separated me
more from society.
My white grandmother was there
despite her prejudices.
I was a human baby.
I did not choose my parents
or my skin color.
I was an innocent child
brought into a world divided by race.
I had done nothing wrong.
My grandmother now saw me in a New Light!
I was her grandson!
I was no ordinary child.
I was a new member of the family.
I was the son of her youngest daughter.
Sometimes people must have a life-changing experience
to see things in a New Light!

Andrew Lytle

My Soul and I

My soul and I had a frank discussion
but then it turned to an argument
We had to separate across the room.
I went to a corner to brood, and he
faced the wall and sulked.

My heart and I, we realized,
we love each other but it might
be better if we saw some other people.
We shook hands, it was real
friendly, kisses on the cheeks for
everyone, hearty handshakes all around.

Now my money makes me complete
by being the perfect jigsaw piece.
It has so many more colors than a soul,
and when it cracks, it's easier to replace
than a heart. It's more logical, economical,
and surprisingly, warm.

Warmer when it burns.

Kirk Alexander

Cadenza

To My Friend

I remember you.
With blonde hair that fell to your knees—
I wanted hair like that.
So thick and straight
Like those women from the Pantene Pro-V commercials.

Then one day you came to school
With it all pulled away into a lump at the back of your head,
Shining through the black netting like
A pirate's hidden bag of gold.

I begged you to please take it down and
You looked at me with defeated eyes that peered out from behind
long willow-tree eyelashes
And said you could not.
I asked why, you explained
"It's the Muslim way."

I went home and cried for your golden hair,
Buried like a black sin at your neck.

Your father was not like mine,
Who dropped me off at the movies.
Yours scolded you when you simply asked.
As I brushed my wild, knotty hair,
Your mother folded yours into a bun.

Secured it tightly.

Jennifer Kiilerich

Subway

He sits on a bench on a subway platform,
watching the smoke rise off the tracks.
The icy bitterness of winter
has dried the rough skin covering his hands
that now crack and bleed at the joints.
His hair is caked and twisted;
he is adorned with tattered clothes,
worn beyond any recognizable color,
too dirty,
too brittle,
too old to provide any kind of comfort from the cold.
Screeching trains open their doors,
pouring out the morning crowds
to wash over him as they scurry
to their destinations.
The city comes alive,
surging with the life of a new day.
The man sits idly,
a glimmer reflecting in his glassy eyes
as he watches smoke rise off the tracks.

Aisha Siebert

Cadenza

Lost In St. Petersburg, 1956

In the 1950s
They tackled life
         Like a forbidden fruit,
    Biting into its
Smooth golden flesh,
             Savoring the sweet essence
                      Of youth.
Drowning lazy sunsets in home-made liquor,
        They awakened
             With a familiar headache,
As the afternoon rays
        Peered through the shutters
             Like bright reminders of idleness…
But they didn't care—the post-war generation—
                  Boys and girls
With callused hands
    And eyes as hollow
            As their dreams.

Oh they knew virtue—
Remembered crying and lying
Their way into crowded army
Med-centers, darting off
Into the darkness with smell
Of medicine clinging to their
Matted hair, clutching a can
Of dry soup or a bottle of
Penicillin to their protruding
Ribs under a ragged shirt.

Cadenza

They knew honesty—
Cutting the ration lines and
Stealing raw meat
From their neighbors, dirty-faced,
Foul-mouthed, dragging their
Small skinny bodies through
The crumbling streets, begging...
Coming home to dying, silent
Mothers, frozen corpses
In their eyes. Empty-handed.

And so in the 1950s,
        They knew how to
                Tackle life,
Drink, smoke, tear its gifts
            And reap its scant favors.
Because their souls
      Lay shattered in the dust
            Of their native cities,
And their future got lost
            On some forgotten battlefield,
Yet they were alive...
          If only for a stolen moment.

Lina Kharats

Cadenza

Cheating Time: Sestina for the Eighties

I thought the whole world was Canadian in the eighties.
I walked around my small town saying, "Eh?" all the time.
In the eighties, my mother was still beautiful.
My dad's hair had yet to lose its color.
I thought *Laugh-In* was a new thing,
Vaguely remembered the Challenger, the astronauts who died

In mid-air. Before the mission even lived, they died.
The flames and wreckage of the rocket shaped the eighties.
I wasn't really sure why it was a bad thing,
But since the world screeched to a stop, I knew it was. It
    was a time
When nothing was real to me. I only imagined the color
Of the exploding flash against the empty sky. Almost beautiful.

There were only absolutes to me, and everything was beautiful.
I don't remember when Warhol or Olivier died,
But I wish I did. I remember some things in color
And some in black and white. The eighties
Look like The Wizard of Oz to me, with Madonna this time.
I wanted to be Dangermouse: tinier than anything,

But with power over everything.
And I thought I was. But pink lace was still beautiful.
Everyone was a child then. We had all the time
In the world. We didn't understand AIDS, or those who died
From it. We pretended it would go away, because it was the
    eighties.
Cyndi Lauper just wanted to have fun, and saw our true colors

Cadenza

Shining through. But the colors
Were more muted then. 24 crayons were enough for anything
And vision was still low-res. But in the eighties,
Technology was art; the hulking slow IBMs were beautiful
And the Thanksgiving tea party when Grandpa died—
I didn't know what happened, or that he had just been cheat-
    ing time.

But we'd all gone home by the time
The memories began to fade, along with the colors
Of the photographs and the flowers and the loves that died.
There went Grandma's last good thing.
The house, never really beautiful,
Stood empty but for a widow and the game shows of the
    eighties.

Out of minds and time, day-glo no longer beautiful
We let Dr. Seuss die and went on to the next big thing.
Neon-colored memories, scratched like thrown-out records—
    the last shout (a dying fall) of the eighties.

Sarah Dryden

Cadenza

Never Go to Florida

have you ever been to Florida?
when I was five I went to Florida.
that's where they grow oranges, not those little oranges in
    Mrs. Oakley's backyard
big juicy oranges, the kind that get your shirt all sticky.
it's too bad that I don't really like oranges all that much.
did you know that in Florida they have a beach?
we don't have a beach in Nashville, but I went to the beach
    in Florida.
everybody loves the beach...except me.
it's really hot there and when I get too hot, I break into hives.
something bit my toe
my mom said it was a crab, but it had to be a monster.
do you know what else is in Florida? Disneyland!
my dad said that I would love the Tower of Terror
unfortunately for me and the guy in front of me,
my stomach did not love the Tower of Terror.
that guy was so mad that I had chili for lunch
that he hit my dad in the nose.
we had to go to the hospital.
did you know that I have a girlfriend?
her name is Cynthia and she is in the second grade.
well, she is not really my girlfriend anymore,
when I went to Florida she found out that she didn't like me
    anymore
she likes Jacob Johnson instead.
he is in the third grade.
I think he stole my bike too!
so for anyone going on vacation,
Never go to Florida.

Marchello Gray

We thank our especially generous sponsors for helping us make this book possible:

Butler's Run

THE CUMBERLAND
The Cumberland Apartments

GIARRATANA. L.L.C.   **Hagerty Peterson**

Mr. Granbery Jackson, III   **Pilcher Partners, L P.**

Special thanks to Metro Police Sgt. Jeff Keeter for his generous help and to the Hume Fogg Community of teachers and students for their support in making this publication a reality.

To publish a book for your school or not-for-profit organization that complements your academic and financial goals, please contact

Write Together™ Publishing LLC:

4064 Nolensville Road, PMB #342
Nashville, TN 37211

Phone: 615-781-1518
Fax: 520-223-4850

www.writetogether.com
fundraising@writetogether.com